HELL: PARADISE FOUND

Seth Panitch

BROADWAY PLAY PUBLISHING INC
New York
www.broadwayplaypublishing.com
info@broadwayplaypublishing.com

HELL: PARADISE FOUND
© Copyright 2015 by Seth Panitch

First printing: June 2015
I S B N: 978-0-88145-633-2

Book design: Marie Donovan
Page make-up: Adobe Indesign
Typeface: Palatino
Printed and bound in the U S A

ABOUT THE AUTHOR

Seth Panitch is a playwright, director, actor, and screenwriter. His plays include ALCESTIS ASCENDING (produced off Broadway at the Harold Clurman Theater, and in Havana, Cuba at the Teatro Raquel Revuelta by the Cuban National Office of Scenic Arts); HELL: PARADISE FOUND (produced off Broadway at the 59E59 Theaters and in Los Angeles at the Ventura Court Playhouse); DAMMIT SHAKESPEARE! (produced off Broadway at Urban Stages and the Westbeth Theatre Center, and in Los Angeles at The Globe Theatre); and WHAT'S TAKING MOSES SO LONG? (produced in Los Angeles at the Wooden O).

In 2008, Seth became the first U S director to work in partnership with the Cuban National Office of Scenic Arts when he directed Shakespeare's THE MERCHANT OF VENICE at the Teatro Adolfo Llaurado in Havana, Cuba. He subsequently directed Cuban productions of A MIDSUMMER NIGHT'S DREAM, Christopher Durang's BEYOND THERAPY, and his play ALCESTIS ASCENDING at the Teatro Raquel Revuelta and the Teatro Berthold Brecht. He has also directed off Broadway (Harold Clurman Theatre, 59E59 Theaters, Urban Stages) and at the Colorado and Texas Shakespeare Festivals.

As a performer, Seth has worked off Broadway (59E59 Theaters, Urban Stages, Westbeth Theatre

Center), regionally at the Colorado, Utah and Texas Shakespeare Festivals, and in Los Angeles at the Hillside Repertory Theatre, the Ventura Court Playhouse, The Globe Theatre, Dramatic New Art Theatre, and the Wooden O.

His documentary *A Night in the Theater* has been published by Insight Media, and his second documentary *Company HavanaBama: Directing Across the Gulf* was screened by the 15th annual Sidewalk Film Festival.

Since 2005, Seth has directed the M F A and Undergraduate Acting programs at the University of Alabama, where he was awarded the Burnum Distinguished Faculty Award in 2014, the Alabama National Alumni Association's "Outstanding Commitment to Teaching Award" in 2010, and was named the 2010 Druid Arts Educator of the Year.

Seth received his B A at Occidental College in Los Angeles and an M F A in Acting at the University of Washington's Professional Actor's Training Program.

He is a member of both the Society of Stage Directors and Choreographers and the Dramatists Guild of America, and the Illuminati, although he has steadfastly resisted branding any of their names on his chest.

HELL: PARADISE FOUND had its Los Angeles premiere at the Ventura Court Theatre on 13 October 1997.

The New York premiere was at 59E59 Theatres on 10 July 2012. The cast and creative contributors were:

SIMON ACKERMAN .... Matt Lewis
THE INTERVIEWER .... Seth Panitch
LUCIFER, VLAD THE IMPALER .... Chip Persons
GOD .... Dianne Teague
LIZZIE BORDEN, EVE .... Alexandra Ficken
DON JUAN, ADAM .... Lawson Hangartner
GABRIEL, SHAKESPEARE .... Peyton Conley
MARIA TERESA .... Stacy Panitch

Director .... Seth Panitch
Set & lights .... Brian Elliot
Costumes .... Tiffany Harris
Music .... Raphael Crystal
Choreography .... Stacey Alley

CHARACTERS & SETTING

The People (5M, 3F):

SIMON ACKERMAN *(M)*
THE INTERVIEWER *(M)*
GOD *(F)*
LUCIFER/VLAD THE IMPALER/DAPPER DEVIL/JUDGE *(M)*
DON JUAN/ADAM/ELVIS/HITLER *(M)*
GABRIEL/PROSECUTOR/SINATRA/SHAKESPEARE/
  EINSTEIN *(M)*
EVE/LIZZIE BORDEN/VICTIM/DANCER *(F)*
MOTHER MARIA TERESA/DANCER *(F)*

The Places:

The Interview: Today

The Trial: Yesterday

Happy Hour: Today, a little later

The Music:

Licenses for Let's Fall in Love, I Will Survive *and* All
of Me *can be obtained through Bourne Music Company,
Universal Music Company, and Marlong Music Company,
respectively. The excising of any or all the above musical
numbers is at the discretion of future productions, so
long as written permission has been obtained through the
playwright.*

The Introduction

(Music: A low pulsing. From the darkness, a chorus of sharply whispered warnings:)

VOICES: "Beware/ the Serpent…"
"Beware/ the Satan…"
"Beware/ the Star of Morning…"

VOICE: "Speak of the Devil and he shall appear!"

(A figure appears in the shadows, draped in a black cloak, the high collar masking his features.)

VOICES: "Beware, for the Devil can cite scripture for his purpose… His name is Legion, for he is many… And the great dragon was cast out, that old serpent, Satan, who deceiveth the whole world…"

(Two darkly clad feminine figures materialize beside him, as the whispering builds in intensity. They grasp the sides of his cape…)

VOICES: "…Now the serpent was more subtle than any beast of the field, and he said unto the woman, Yea, hath God not said, Ye shall not eat of *every tree of the garden?*"

(Spotlight on the figure, as he raises his head—)

SHADOWY FIGURE: "Let's…"

(The women yank off his cloak, revealing a dapper well-dressed devil-about-town. He sings a snappy rendition of Let's Fall In Love, *as the lights snap from gloom to glamour…)*

DAPPER DEVIL: "...Fall in Love! Why shouldn't we—fall in love? Our hearts are made of it, let's take a chance, why be afraid of it?"

(DAPPER DEVIL *dances elegantly with the women.*)

DANCING WOMEN: "Let's close our eyes, and make a "Lost Paradise!" Little we know of it, still we can try to make a go of it."

(ALBERT EINSTEIN *and* ADOLPH HITLER *appear, entering with great gravitas.*)

DAPPER DEVIL: "Now, we might have been meant for each other..."

EINSTEIN: "To be—"

HITLER: "Or *Nein* to be—"

EINSTEIN/HITLER: "Let our hearts discover!"

(EINSTEIN *and* HITLER *break into dance...*)

(*The "Elevator" [the women holding two Art Deco doors before the entering* SIMON ACKERMAN] *"descends"...*)

ALL: "Let's fall in love! Why shouldn't we fall in love? Now is the time for it, while we are young..."

(*Ding! The elevator "opens".*)

(SIMON *exits, infinitely confused by the crowd posed before him.*)

DAPPER DEVIL: "Let's fall in love!"

(EINSTEIN *and* HITLER *dance by* SIMON.)

EINSTEIN/HITLER: "Let's fall in love!"

(*All scatter, but look back one last time for:*)

ALL: "Let's fall in love!"

(*The* DAPPER DEVIL *deftly slips back into the shadows [greeting the* INTERVIEWER *on his way in] before he disappears, along with everyone else, save a stupefied* SIMON.)

(The music climaxes, and the lights change into—)

(The interview:)

(A dazzling art deco office. Rich, bright, colors—from a distant, perhaps better, time and place. A deep red rosewood desk, a rather imposing file cabinet behind, a lone chair across the stage…)

(The INTERVIEWER, *smartly dressed, crisp, curious, sits expectantly behind the desk with a wide grin. Although surrounded by the accoutrements of office, this is not the kind of man who revels in bureaucracy. Not the kind of man who reads Civil Code Books on the toilet. He continues smiling expectantly at* SIMON, *who remains before him, and remains confused…)*

SIMON: Hi.

INTERVIEWER: *(Pause)* Hello.

SIMON: *(Pause)* I'm sorry. I'm a little confused. I think I'm—

INTERVIEWER: Lost? You're not. Not that there's anything wrong with that, if that is indeed your preference… *(Fishing through files)* Mister… Uh…

SIMON: Acker—

INTERVIEWER: Please don't tell me. *(Still searching)* Where the hell did I… Ah! Found it. *(He brandishes a thin file.)*

INTERVIEWER: Mister Ackerman. *(Hesitates)* Simon Ackerman.

SIMON: Yes. That's me. How did you…?

INTERVIEWER: Come on in, Simon. Take a seat. How about some coffee?

SIMON: I'm sorry, I missed your name. You are…

INTERVIEWER: I really don't think you could pronounce it. I have *other* names, of course, names you probably *could* pronounce, but they mean different things to you then they do to me, so I'd just as soon not use them. But your name—very distinctive. *(Beat)* What was it? *(Checking the file)* Oh yes, "Simon Ackerman." Ooo. I like that. "Simon Acker-man." Oh, I like the *sound* of that. I think I shall call myself "Simon Ackerman" from now on.

SIMON: You can't do that. I'm Simon Ackerman.

INTERVIEWER: Not anymore. I'm Simon Ackerman— you go be someone else for a while.

SIMON: I will not. I like who I am.

INTERVIEWER: Well, you know what they say— "Too much of a good thing… Lest it corrupt…" DAMN! Never could remember that. Tennyson. Not my favorite, but what an original. Not as original as E. E. Cummings, but I never understood what the hell *he* was all about in the first place, so let's talk about Tennyson, shall we?

Simon stares at him.

SIMON: I think I'd like that coffee now.

INTERVIEWER: Sorry, don't have any.

SIMON: But—

INTERVIEWER: I know. I'm sorry. I lied. Compulsive liar. Lot of them around here. Lot of Artists, you know— "create your own reality." *(He chuckles.)* Up *there*, well. Up there, there is only *one* reality. And they love it. Like one big happy school of fish. How can they stand it?

SIMON: …Up there?

INTERVIEWER: Yes. Up there. *(Whispers) Heaven.* God help 'em.

SIMON: …Heaven? Did you say Heaven?

INTERVIEWER: Terribly sorry. Nirvana, Vallhalla, Elysian Fields—I did not mean to assume you were Judeo-Christian.

SIMON: Heaven.

(The INTERVIEWER *nods)*

SIMON: Up there.

(The INTERVIEWER *nods again.)*

SIMON: Then where am I?

(The INTERVIEWER *just smiles.)*

(Simon rises, terrified.)

SIMON: That's impossible!

INTERVIEWER: Oh, fine—two seconds ago Heaven was just a nod and a whisper away, but Hell so much as gets *implied* and we're in the middle of a John Carpenter film.

SIMON: *(Dubiously)* Alright, then—if this is Hell, where are your horns?

INTERVIEWER: *(Playing along)* Lost 'em in a poker game.

SIMON: Leathery wings?

INTERVIEWER: Dry cleaners.

SIMON: Pitchfork?

INTERVIEWER: This is *Hell*, Simon, not Hollywood— although the two are intimately connected according to the Republican National Convention.

SIMON: You must be joking.

INTERVIEWER: Oh no. I don't joke. I *lie*.

SIMON: You must be mistaken!

INTERVIEWER: No, really. I can't tell a joke. It's awful. Something about my, you know… *(Huge pause)* … timing.

SIMON: I don't understand. There must be some mistake. I'm...I'm a Religious Man.

INTERVIEWER: *(Beat)* Well, what is *that* supposed to mean?

SIMON: I'm a Religious Man.

INTERVIEWER: Are you implying that we discriminate?

SIMON: Excuse me?

INTERVIEWER: That we discriminate. Against Religious Men. That because you're a Religious Man, that somehow takes you out of the running?

SIMON: No, I—

INTERVIEWER: *(Standing)* How *dare* you, sir!

SIMON: What?

INTERVIEWER: How *dare* you! How dare you walk into my office and toss around words like "discrimination".

SIMON: But, I didn't—

INTERVIEWER: I approach every case with an open mind! I consider all the facts! I am equal and fair in my judgment!

SIMON: I'm sorry. I—please let me speak! *(Pause)* I'm sorry. I did not mean to imply that you had prejudged me. I...I'm awfully confused right now. You say I am in Hell. I don't remember *dying*.

(INTERVIEWER takes a peek at the file.)

INTERVIEWER: Sushi.

SIMON: I don't understand. I was eaten by an angry flounder?

INTERVIEWER: *(Laughing)* No, of course not— although what a way to go. No, you ate some bad sushi at... *(Reading)* Bento Sushi on University.

SIMON: That's it?

INTERVIEWER: Apparently so.

SIMON: That's all it says?

INTERVIEWER: Yup. "Cause of Death... Bad sushi."

SIMON: *(Floored)* Wow.

INTERVIEWER: Yeah. Life is cheap. Apparently, sushi isn't. Says here you were overcharged—

SIMON: But so suddenly.

INTERVIEWER: Well, that's death, for you. Everything's A-O K, and then suddenly...

SIMON: *(Gravely)* Heaven or Hell.

INTERVIEWER: Depending on your record.

SIMON: So, this is a *trial*?

INTERVIEWER: Not exactly. I like to think of this as an Interview. You see this— *(Holds up file)* —is a record of every thing you've ever done—

(SIMON stares at the file.)

SIMON: It's awfully thin.

INTERVIEWER: Oh, Simon, it's not the size of the record, it's what you've done with it. Take James Dean—

(INTERVIEWER tosses SIMON a tiny file.)

SIMON: This is...this is very small.

INTERVIEWER: Yes, but what an original. So, you see, Simon, you have no less of a chance than James Dean.

SIMON: To...?

INTERVIEWER: Why, to get into Hell, of course!

SIMON: But I don't want to go to Hell. I want to go to Heaven.

INTERVIEWER: *(Sighs)* Oh dear, oh dear, oh dear. *(He makes a note in SIMON's file.)*

SIMON: What?

INTERVIEWER: "What fools these mortals be."

SIMON: What are you talking about?

INTERVIEWER: Shakespeare. He's here. Interesting coincidence—he just wrote a play for James Dean. Poor James. Verse is just *not* his thing.

SIMON: *(Realizing)* You're tempting me!

INTERVIEWER: Sorry?

SIMON: You're *tempting* me, right? Like Adam or Eve or Linda Blair! *(Gaining confidence)* Well, you can just cut it out right now, mister, because... *(Standing)* BECAUSE I BELIEVE IN GOD!

INTERVIEWER: *(Unimpressed)* Uh huh...

SIMON: And I deny your dominion over my soul!

INTERVIEWER: Please sit down Mister Ackerman.

SIMON: Don't tempt me with your pleasantries, Demon! I've read all about your kind!

(The INTERVIEWER ends the interview cordially.)

INTERVIEWER: Thank you. *(He makes a few notes and signs with a flourish.)*

SIMON: What?

INTERVIEWER: Thank you. I have all I need.

SIMON: You do...? What do you—

INTERVIEWER: Thank you. Please close the door on the way out.

SIMON: But...where do I go?

INTERVIEWER: You go to Heaven. Isn't that what you want?

SIMON: You mean—I can go?

INTERVIEWER: Certainly. What's to stop you?

(SIMON bolts to the door. Halts)

SIMON: Excuse me—how exactly do I...?

INTERVIEWER: Terribly sorry. Down the hall, past the Monet, take a right, you'll see a big escalator. There'll be a couple of Angels, and if you're lucky, they won't be singing. There's a guy at the top in a plain blue sportcoat named Saint Peter. You can call him Saint Peter—or Peter, he really has no preference. About anything. It's awful. Like talking to a weather vane. Unless you bring up *fish*. Whatever you do, *don't*, or he'll talk your ear off until the End of Days. *(Beat)* I digress. Give him this.

(INTERVIEWER hands the file to SIMON.)

SIMON: Thank you.

INTERVIEWER: Sure. "Have a nice eternity."

(SIMON goes to the door. Turns back)

SIMON: Sorry about the "Demon" thing.

INTERVIEWER: Oh, don't worry about that. Happens all the time. One gets used to it.

SIMON: I meant no disrespect. I'm sure you make a wonderful Demon.

INTERVIEWER: I'm not a Demon, Mister Ackerman...I am a *Bureaucrat*. In Hell, all Demons are Bureaucrats. On Earth, all Bureaucrats are Demons.

(SIMON glances down at the file.)

SIMON: It says "rejected"!

INTERVIEWER: Yes. Sorry about that.

SIMON: But, I thought I made it. To Heaven.

INTERVIEWER: You did.

SIMON: Then what am I rejected from?

INTERVIEWER: From Hell.

(INTERVIEWER *returns to his work.* SIMON *remains, suspicious…*)

SIMON: But…don't you want my soul?

INTERVIEWER: *(Beat)* Now why on Earth would I want that?

SIMON: To punish me…for my transgressions. Put me to work…you know, in the…fire pits.

INTERVIEWER: In the… Oh, Simon! You've been reading far too much Milton. You'll do very well "up there". In Heaven, everyone reads Milton.

(SIMON *crosses in to the* INTERVIEWER.*)*

SIMON: Why do you continue to refer to Heaven as if it's a prison? Heaven is paradise! It's rapture! It's ecstasy!

INTERVIEWER: It's *boring!*

SIMON: Boring? Now I know you're lying. Good day, Sir! Heaven boring? Right! *(He flies out the door.)*

INTERVIEWER: *(Checking his watch)* Five, four, three, two—

(SIMON *bursts back in.*)

SIMON: And if it *is* boring, and I am sure it is *not*, but if it *is* boring, then that is…well, then that is the way it is *supposed* to be.

INTERVIEWER: Well, "the Lord works in mysterious ways."

SIMON: He certainly does. *(Beat)* What do you mean by that?

(*The* INTERVIEWER *emerges from behind the desk.*)

INTERVIEWER: Just that I wonder why it is always so damn difficult for you Humans to explain Divine actions, but so easy for you to explain Demonic ones?

SIMON: I don't know.

INTERVIEWER: I'll tell you. It is because Human nature is closer to the Demonic. It always has been. It always will be.

(SIMON *comes back into the room.*)

SIMON: Well, you'll get no argument from me there. In my line of work, my Old Line, I guess—I was a lawyer, a defense lawyer to be precise—should I still call myself a lawyer...?

INTERVIEWER: You? *Absolutely.*

SIMON: Well, as a lawyer, you realize pretty quickly that humanity is basically equal parts incompetence and sin.

INTERVIEWER: Uhgh— "Sin." You Humans toss that word around as if it were some cosmic hot potato. You're *dead.* What does it matter now? How much money can you steal from Hercules? The guy doesn't even carry a wallet. 'Course if he did—where would he *put* the damn thing—his toga's tighter than a tourniquet. Have you *seen* his physique in the last thousand years? And to siphon himself in like that? Now *that's* a Sin! Forget Sin. Sin has nothing to do with anything. You will see just as many sinners in Heaven as in Hell.

SIMON: Sinners in Heaven? Shakespeare in Hell? You're lying—you have to be. Heaven is for the blest—and Hell the damned!

INTERVIEWER: *(Deadly serious)* On the contrary! Heaven is for *sheep*—Hell is for the *shepherd*! *(Pause)* Who do you suppose goes to Heaven, anyway? *Anyone.* Anyone goes to Heaven. Anyone who follows another lead, anyone who defers to another explanation, anyone who believes because they are told to believe, or drinks Coke because they're told to drink Coke, or stops questioning because they are told to "have faith!" The Establishment, The Company Man, The Girl Next Door; The Hardliner, The Party Liner, The General Public; The Pulpit, the Moshpit, the "I'll Just *Take* a Hit;" Fashionistas, Moralizers, Twitterizers, Electric Sliders, Hip-Hoppers, White Rappers, Song Samplers, Moon-Walkers; Multi Taskers, Talking Pointers, Focus Groupers, Facebookers! *These* are the ones damned to an eternity of faith, following orders, conformity, and consistency!

(Silence)

SIMON: *(Skeptically)* Assuming this is true... Who goes to Hell?

INTERVIEWER: Everyone else. *(Sitting)* But Hell is a minority; a dwindling, dwindling minority. Our standards are quite simply just too high. You see, Heaven is for the disciple. Hell is for the Christ.

SIMON: Jesus? In *Hell*?

INTERVIEWER: Oh no. *(Chuckles)* No, no, no. We *wanted* him, though. He visits from time to time. Not a great singer...but what an *original*. *(He removes a large remote and a bowl of popcorn from his desk.)*

SIMON: What are you doing?

INTERVIEWER: I think I can clear this up for you, once and for all. You like going to the movies, Simon?

SIMON: Sure.

INTERVIEWER: Then you are going to love this! *(Pointing the remote)* You know something? I've seen this Eight Hundred Million times, and it just keeps getting better *every* time I watch it! *(He offers SIMON some popcorn.)* Popcorn?

SIMON: Is it airpopped?

INTERVIEWER: What are you—on a diet? You're dead man, live a little! *(He pushes a button on the remote, and…)*

(Blackout. Wagner—classical and grand…)

The Trial

(Lights up on Heaven's Supreme, and only, Court. There is a large gold imposing throne in the middle of the chamber. Down stage right is a small bench—long enough to support two people.)

(The Archangel GABRIEL *sits on the throne, "playing God" to an imaginary court. His dress suggests a Nineteenth Century Romanticism—elegant, poetic, and reasoned.* GABRIEL *looks the overachiever—an angel that has risen to his position of power through hard work and diligence, not talent.)*

(Suddenly, the calm of the chamber is broken by the tortured entrance of ADAM. GABRIEL *leaps from the throne so as not to be spotted upon it.* ADAM *appears a young, extremely attractive boy-man in his early twenties. His dress is also of this Pseudo-Romantic period, but it hangs uncomfortably over his lanky frame.)*

ADAM: Oh Gabriel! Gabriel! I am undone!

Adam throws himself onto the floor. Gabriel rushes to him.

GABRIEL: Courage Adam. You have nothing to fear. What God does, God does out of *love* for you and Eve.

ADAM: Oh, if you could have seen God's *face*. The anguish. The disappointment. I broke God's heart, Gabriel! God gave me life, and I gave thanks by spitting in God's holy face!

GABRIEL: Take hold of yourself, Adam, you must!

ADAM: *Eve*—that beast! She *made* me. She made me
eat that apple. "Try it. You'll Like it," she says. And
here I am, my soul in peril, and for *what*? It didn't even
taste that good. It was so tart. She knows I prefer the
sweet ones. *(Sobs)* Oh, Gabriel, what have I done? *(He
collapses at* GABRIEL's *feet, as…)*

*(*EVE *enters. The First Woman. Natural, Sexual, Noble. Her
dress is lovely, but confines the beauty beneath.)*

EVE: Adam!

*(*ADAM *freezes, his arms wrapped about* GABRIEL's *ankles.
She looks down, thoroughly disgusted.)*

EVE: What precisely in your constitution compels you
to kneel before every minor deity in the Cosmos?

GABRIEL: *(Crossing in, offended) Minor*? I'll have you
know, Woman, that in terms of Mortal Awe, I out-poll
99.981% of the celestial beings in the Firmament.

(Ignoring GABRIEL, EVE *has crossed to* ADAM, *joining him
on her knees.)*

EVE: Dear Lord—what is the point of the fibula and
tibia if Man refuses to use any bone beneath the
patella?

*(*ADAM *quickly stands, dusting himself off.)*

ADAM: That's untrue, Eve. I use these bones as often, or
more often, than any other bone in my body!

*(*EVE *sighs on her knees, staring at* ADAM's *crotch.)*

EVE: I am all too aware of that Adam, to my eternal
disappointment.

(Music: heroic, soaring, regal. Ride of the Valkyries, *only
grander…)*

(All three bow to the ground.)

*(*GOD *[a woman] enters in the majestic dress of an
Enlightened Queen—the Sun Queen, literally. She strolls*

*happily past the assembled group, right out the door. All
continue to freeze.)*

(After a moment, GOD *peeks back in. Fascinated, she creeps
back into the room, mounts her throne, and gestures to
an above stage light, which immediately bathes her in a
heavenly glow. She seems very pleased by everything…)*

GABRIEL: *(Delicately)* My Lord?

GOD: Hmm? *(Beat, realizing)* Oh, yes. Sorry. *(Clears Her
throat)* I AM THAT I AM.

(All rise. ADAM *and* EVE *sit on the bench.* GABRIEL *slides
over to God's side.)*

GABRIEL: *Very* impressive, my Lord.

GOD: Thank you, Gabe. I've been working on it.

GABRIEL: Very commanding, my Lord.

GOD: Can you hear the compassion as well—

GABRIEL: Oh yes—

GOD: I've been working on the compassion.

GABRIEL: Very compassionate.

GOD: It's not *too* compassionate? I'd hate to lose the
authority.

GABRIEL: Oh no, I can hear the authority. I can hear it
quite clearly.

GOD: *(Hopefully)* You're not just saying that?

GABRIEL: Oh no, my Lord! Very commanding…in a
compassionate but authoritative manner.

GOD: Thank you, Gabe! Thank you *very* much! Thank
you! *(She begins to leave.)*

GABRIEL: My Lord…?

GOD: Hmm?

GABRIEL: Where are you going?

GOD: *(Beat)* I have absolutely *no* idea.

GABRIEL: I believe you called for the High Court to be assembled.

GOD: *(Fascinated)* Really? Why?

GABRIEL: I believe it had something to do with the Satan Matter.

GOD: What's the matter with Satan?

GABRIEL: No, my Lord—don't you wish to deal with Satan?

GOD: Why? What's he done?

(GABRIEL shows the apple, with two large bites in it.)

GOD: Oh yes! Sorry about that. Don't know *where* my mind is today. I should have made *today* the Sabbath and taken a rest, eh, Gabriel?

GABRIEL: As you wish, my Lord. *(He puts down the apple, and begins to write it down in the Book Of Law.)*

GOD: Oh no, Gabriel. Just kidding. Just kidding, Gabriel. *(Sits)* Big mistake not giving the Angels a sense of humor.

GABRIEL: My Lord?

GOD: Nothing, Gabriel. Send him in. Send in…my Satan.

GABRIEL: Send in the prisoner!

(Music: A dark, ominous march)

(LUCIFER enters, his hands in shackles. He is dressed similarly to GABRIEL, but with a singular dashing flair. GABRIEL removes the shackles and withdraws to GOD's side.)

GABRIEL: Please state your name before the court.

LUCIFER: I am Lucifer.

GABRIEL: Please state your *given* name. The *title* God has chosen for you.

LUCIFER: I pray you have not convened this Holy Court to fathom my preference of names, Gabriel. But if this is indeed the weighty matter before us, I am called the Lord's Satan, her Protector, but my *name* is Lucifer.

GOD: *(Hiding a thin grin)* Well said, Lucifer. Please continue, Archangel.

GABRIEL: The charges, sir, are heresy, dissent, subversion, wanton temptation and willful disobedience.

LUCIFER: Well, I have been busy, haven't I?

GABRIEL: Are you aware of the severity of these charges?

LUCIFER: I am now, thanks to the ominous tone in which you pronounced them.

GABRIEL: And how do you plead?

LUCIFER: Guilty.

(Commotion)

GOD: Satan! *(Regaining her composure)* To say Guilty is to say you willfully disobeyed Us. Think again, and think clearly of your answer. Gabriel, ask again.

GABRIEL: Did you, or did you not, tempt God's creation Eve to eat of the Tree of Knowledge, an act reserved solely for Archangels of the Lord?

(All lean in, expectantly...)

LUCIFER: I did.

(Commotion)

(EVE bursts up out of her seat.)

EVE: This proceeding is a sham!

(LUCIFER ties to block her from GOD.)

LUCIFER: Eve!

EVE: I never requested this—

LUCIFER: I never sought your permission—

(GABRIEL *yanks* EVE *away from* LUCIFER.)

GABRIEL: Mind yourself, Woman, you are in the Court of the Lord.

EVE: Mind your hands, Gabriel, or I shall bite them off.

(GABRIEL *retires.*)

GABRIEL: You heard that—you all heard that! Threatening a superior being!

(All stare.)

GABRIEL: ME! She threatened *me*! I'm the superior being! *(Losing whatever composure he still had)* You all know that, and it's time you started treating me that way!

GOD: Gabriel, heel.

(GABRIEL *"heels" to* GOD's *side.)*

GOD: Now, Eve, I do admire your enthusiasm, but I can't have every creation running around Heaven screaming at the top of their lungs. We'll never get a thing accomplished.

EVE: Forgive me, my Lord, but I coveted that apple!

(Commotion)

EVE: I wanted it, my Lord! I wasn't tricked, I wasn't tempted—I was intrigued. I knew, within that Apple… lay Knowledge.

GOD: *(Warmly)* I give you Knowledge, Eve.

EVE: You give it second hand, My Lord. I wanted it *first* hand—uncensored, undiluted. *(Crossing to* LUCIFER*)* So I came to your Satan, your Guardian, as he stood watch at the Tree of Knowledge. I begged him to let me eat of its fruit, and as much as I know that it pained him to do so, he did what he did for *pity*, not for disobedience. I am the Tempter! And it is I that should be held in contempt of your Law!

(Commotion)

GOD: Lucifer, is this true?

LUCIFER: It is not, my Lord.

GABRIEL: *(Pressing him)* You deny her testimony? You deny Eve's sworn testimony?

LUCIFER: *(Exploding)* I deny that it pained me to surrender that Tree. It troubled me not a whit. I do assent that I pitied Eve, as I do still, as I do all God's creations. As I do Her.

Commotion.

GOD: *(Flabbergasted) Pity* me? Did he—did you say...? I am *above* pity. I am above rebuke. "I Am That I Am."

LUCIFER: You are that you are, my lord, but you are not what you *think*!

(The assembly freezes, shocked.)

(GOD walks directly up to a hushed LUCIFER.)

GOD: Is that so, Lucifer? Have you so sounded my very spirit? Am I, and all that I am, now open to your interpretation? Perhaps, lest I lose all my Mystery, I should endeavor to provide you the occasional surprise. *(Turns to EVE)* Eve, come forward.

LUCIFER: My Lord—!

(GOD halts LUCIFER with a single look.)

(EVE steps forward, as GOD circles about her.)

GOD: Eve, in addition to my earlier decree, casting you out of Eden and withdrawing the blessings of Eternal life, I shall greatly multiply your pain and travail; in pain thou shalt bring forth children; and thy desire shall be to thy husband, and…let's see—what to do, what to do…ah! *(For* LUCIFER*)* He shall *rule* over thee.

EVE: *(Turning to* ADAM*)* He shall *rule* over me?

ADAM: *(Thrilled)* I shall *rule* over her?

GOD: You shall.

*(*ADAM *gloats.)*

GOD: Without gloating.

*(*ADAM *halts)*

GOD: Withdraw.

*(*GOD *sits.* ADAM *places his arm around her. She shudders.)*

*(*GOD *contentedly returns to the throne, as:)*

LUCIFER: My Lord, bethink yourself—

GOD: I have, Lucifer. You might do the same, before your words condemn them to an even greater chastisement.

LUCIFER: *Why*, my Lord? Why punish the desire for knowledge? Is there anything purer in the Universe?

GOD: Yes, Lucifer—obedience. A line has been crossed.

LUCIFER: Are you surprised? "Every tree in Eden *except* the Tree of Knowledge?" Why? You wouldn't give them stomachs and refuse to feed them. You wouldn't give them eyes and make them blind. Why do you *tease* them so? What has God to fear from Knowledge?

GOD: I do not fear knowledge, Lucifer. I *bestow* it. I bestow it when my creations are *prepared* for it.

LUCIFER: Knowledge is not knowledge when it is handed down from a mountain, my Lord, it is a commandment.

*(*GABRIEL *steps between them.)*

GABRIEL: Now, you keep away from Commandments, Satan. A good Commandment is a precious thing. It brings order to Chaos.

LUCIFER: It brings *your* order to Chaos, isn't that the point?

GABRIEL: It brings *God's* order, *that's* the point. What would you rather—disrupt all Heaven? Would you overthrow God?

LUCIFER: I would do no such thing. I love God more than your toady minion heart could ever understand.

GOD: More of *that*, Lucifer! You are finally on to something there.

LUCIFER: God is good. I know She is—as sure as I know you are a mindless matrix of moronism fit only for legislative governance, which is, in practice, a not so subtle form of group masturbation—so I would watch that, if I were you.

(GABRIEL *backs off.*)

LUCIFER: Yes, God is good. But that Throne She sits in is *Evil*!

(Commotion. In his growing rage, LUCIFER kicks the side of the throne.)

LUCIFER: Evil, I say! That throne *demands*. It demands She be infallible, pure as Space. It forbids Her to trust. How can She? For the moment the sheep can come home without assistance… *(Turns to* GOD, *realizing)* … The Shepherd is out of a job!

(Commotion)

GOD: SATAN! I command your silence! *(Silence)* Have you heard of Hell?

LUCIFER: *(Beat)* I have my Lord.

GOD: Are you aware I have decreed all Heretics shall be consigned to its cavernous depths?

LUCIFER: I was *not*, My Lord.

GOD: Then listen very closely to what *I* have to say—it is *my* turn to speak! I am prepared to forgive you this unfair, unprovoked, unimaginable outburst, if you are prepared to recant all that you have said, and take your rightful place once again as my Satan.

LUCIFER: *(Hesitates)* It is a very difficult thing you ask, My Lord. My eyes have been opened.

GOD: Then you will have to shut them, and shut them tight! In spite of all your endless chattering, I tell you knowledge is a dangerous thing. It is all very well for you, an *Archangel*, to stand there and shout about the "Necessity of Knowledge," but look at Man. Look at him!

(GOD *motions and* ADAM *awkwardly stands.)*

GOD: What do you think of him, Lucifer? Is he a vessel for the Knowledge of the Universe, or will it burst him like a bubble? And as for the Woman...

(GOD *motions,* EVE *stands.)*

GOD: She does appear more capable, but not by much.

(GOD *gestures and* ADAM *and* EVE *both sit.)*

GOD: What would you have me do, Lucifer? Pump them full of divinity until they explode? Destroy them in the name of Progress? I take pity on Man when I take his leash, and show him Heavenly compassion when I lead him to where I want him to go. It is a dubious, dangerous question mark you propose, and I am not prepared to bet the future of my creation on the *possibility* of progression.

LUCIFER: But how will you truly know, if you never give them the *chance*? Are you, the Lord God, prepared to spend eternity with that question mark?

GOD: I am. I *will*. *(Pause)* You have your choice. Heaven or Hell. Choose, or be Damned.

Silence. All await his answer...

LUCIFER: I choose Heaven.

GOD: *(Greatly relieved)* O Lucifer, I am overjoyed! Gabriel, make up a deed of apology.

GABRIEL: It is already done, My Lord.

GOD: Good boy! Lucifer, will you sign it?

LUCIFER: I will my Lord.

(LUCIFER goes to GABRIEL to sign the paper. GABRIEL has to give LUCIFER his back for the signing. LUCIFER finishes his signature with a flourish, stinging GABRIEL.)

(GOD grabs the paper from GABRIEL. Reads it)

GOD: Well. You have saved your soul, Satan, and proved yourself most wise. But—and isn't there always a "but" —your previous actions have proven you a grave and undeniable danger to my Creation below. I am sorry Satan, but you have left me no alternative. You yourself are banned from Eden forever. You may not walk the Earth and view Creation. You are consigned to Heaven, and to such an existence as I see fit. *(She turns and walks back to her throne.)*

LUCIFER: *(Distraught)* Consigned to Heaven? Am I never to view Creation again?

(GOD turns back at the base of the dais...)

GOD: *(Laughing)* That's all I need: a race of *you* running around creation, yammering about Knowledge.

LUCIFER: Am I not to be set free?

GOD: Set free? After that torrent of profanation? What do you think me? A complete fool? *(She turns and reascends her dais, with her back to* LUCIFER.*)*

LUCIFER: You would not imprison me! You created me! You created me to *question*!

GOD: *(Spinning back, harshly)* I created you to *OBEY*!

LUCIFER: Give me that paper!

*(*LUCIFER *grabs the paper from* GOD's *outstretched hand and begins ripping it.)*

LUCIFER: Cast me in your Pit. Do you think I fear it as much as I fear a life on a leash? Bring on your Hell!

GABRIEL: *(Warning him)* Satan—take care, your soul—

LUCIFER: My soul be damned. What use have I of soul? My soul is nothing without my *liberty*!

GOD: You will obey me, Satan! You will obey me!

LUCIFER: You call me Lucifer! I am Satan no more!

GOD: You will obey me!

*(*LUCIFER *spins on* GOD, *lashing out:)*

LUCIFER: I will obey *myself*! I will choose. I will question. I will challenge Heaven itself, day after day after week after year until the last whispered breath of the Universe! I will deny every gospel, I will draw my own conclusions. I will assault every assertion, I will interrogate every teacher. I will doubt the doubtless, I will dispute the indisputable, I will object to the unobjectionable, I will *protest*! You say "You are that You are," but I say I am that *I* am, not that You are or that You *want* me to be. Throw me in your Pit, damn me to your Hell—I promise you it shall be a Protestors' *Paradise*, where I shall defend your Creation from You, your Jealousies, your Law, and your Apocalyptic Contradictions!

(A Long Silence)

GOD: How you have fallen, O Lucifer, Son of the Morning. I condemn you to the deepest depths of Hell. You want a Protestors' Paradise? You *build* one! You and any Angel that wishes to join you can protest each other until the end of Time, for all I care.

LUCIFER: And what about Man?

GOD: What about him? You think Humanity wants anything to do with you? You flatter yourself, Lucifer. More importantly, you flatter them. Adam will be their Father.

LUCIFER: And Eve will be their Mother.

GOD: *(Sighs)* Oy. I see your point. Well. What do you propose?

LUCIFER: Let them choose. Let their actions on Earth determine their Eternity. Let them *choose.*

GOD: They don't *know* enough to choose.

LUCIFER: Do they know too much to choose *you?*

GOD: *(Beat, she smiles)* Very well, Lucifer. I accept your challenge! I still think you're wasting your time, but I suppose it's the least I can do—casting you out of Heaven and all.

(GOD stands. ADAM and EVE stand. GOD hesitates.)

GOD: You know the way, I presume?

LUCIFER: Of course. The way to Hell is easy. It is the initial step that is so hard.

(GOD nods. Moves to the exit. Hesitates)

GOD: In spite of this awful mess, I can't help admitting I miss you already. Am I allowed to say that?

LUCIFER: *(Reverently)* Of course you are—you're God.

GOD: *(Without a trace of joy)* I Am. I am indeed. *(Pause)* Well… That's that, then…isn't it?

(GOD exits. Silence)

GABRIEL: You should be ashamed of yourself.

LUCIFER: I am indeed, Gabriel. I have broken Her heart.

GABRIEL: I could—if you wanted…I could *speak* to Her, you know.

LUCIFER: There is no remedy, brother. It is a fundamental chasm. All the apologies in the Firmament cannot bridge it now.

(GABRIEL, hurt, grabs the tray with the apple.)

GABRIEL: You and your big mouth.

(As LUCIFER leaves, he swipes the apple. He turns to find ADAM and EVE waiting.)

LUCIFER: *(To ADAM)* I don't imagine you understand what just transpired?

ADAM: Not a word.

LUCIFER: Bless you, you will lead a very happy life.

(LUCIFER tosses the apple to EVE. Turns to leave. EVE follows.)

LUCIFER: What are you doing?

EVE: I want to follow you.

LUCIFER: *(Gently)* How dare you follow *anyone*. Do what you will, and we shall meet again, I promise you.

(LUCIFER kisses EVE's hand. As they part, he retains his hold on her hand. For a moment the gesture seems quite familiar—it is the mirror image of God's creation of Adam by Michelangelo in the Sistine Chapel.)

(LUCIFER walks to the exit. Turns)

LUCIFER: Farewell, Eve, I must hurry down to Hell—I am expecting quite a lot of company.

(Music)

*(*LUCIFER *exits.)*

(Lights down to ADAM, EVE *and the apple.)*

*(*EVE *offers* ADAM *a bite. He demurs.)*

*(*EVE *shrugs. Takes a huge bite.)*

(Lights fade out…)

The Interview II

(Lights up. Music fades.)

(The INTERVIEWER *is in tears.)*

INTERVIEWER: I'm sorry. It's just like "King Kong." No matter how many times I see it, in the end I'm reduced to a blathering idiot.

SIMON: I'm shocked, I'm surprised, I…I don't know what to say. So there are no fire pits?

INTERVIEWER: *(Blowing his nose)* Oh I never said *that.* There *are* fire pits—but only for those who request them.

SIMON: I don't understand…if there's no punishment or paradise… What does it really matter?

INTERVIEWER: It matters *everything*! Punishment and Paradise mean different things to different people. Remember Sartre, my friend: If Hell is simply other people…then so must be Heaven. The question becomes: in which group do you wish to spend eternity?

SIMON: I see. I appreciate your concern. And it's not that you don't make a good case—you do—you make a very convincing one. It's just—if you separate the Universe into the complacent and the complicated…

I sort of tend towards the complacent. I want to go to Heaven. I'm sorry.

INTERVIEWER: Oh, don't be sorry, Mister Ackerman. It is I that should be sorry. You wanted to go, and I insisted on bending your ears. *(Pause)* That *is* odd, though. Why didn't I just let you leave? What is it about you? What am I missing?

SIMON: Perhaps—

INTERVIEWER: Shut up, I'm speaking rhetorically here! *(Grabs* SIMON's *file)* There is *something* about you, Mister Ackerman. There is definitely something there—I'm just not sure what it is. I only know it is there…somewhere…submerged under all that flabby mediocrity. I can smell it. *(Sniffs)* Oh yes, I can smell it from here. I wish I could tell you that you will be happy in Heaven, and I do not wish to sound cryptic, but… I am not so sure.

SIMON: All my life I wondered if it existed. And now, to be told it does, and to get there, I need only make the decision to go…I don't think there's anything you could say or do to convince me otherwise.

(The INTERVIEWER *shrugs. Offers* SIMON *his file—his ticket into Heaven.* SIMON *takes it and goes, unwittingly leaving a page in Interviewer's hands.)*

INTERVIEWER: No, you forgot— *(Reads the page)* Well, damn my soul all over again, what have we here?!!

SIMON: What?

INTERVIEWER: *(To no one in particular)* You sneaky little Devil!

SIMON: Excuse me?

INTERVIEWER: Not you, Simon. Come on. *(He bolts toward the door.)*

SIMON: Where're we going? I want to—

INTERVIEWER: I know, I know, I know—you want to go to Heaven, blah, blah, blah. Look, Simon—I've got a sneaking suspicion—no, a downright intuitive revelation that you are about to make a mistake of Biblical proportions. Come on, Simon—it's time for you to meet "The Big Boss".

SIMON: Which "Big Boss" is that?

INTERVIEWER: Oh Simon—there's only one Big Boss... That sneaky little devil!

SIMON: I don't know. I've sort of made up my mind, here—

INTERVIEWER: *(At the door)* Simon! Come on! The Redcoats are coming! *(He hangs a sign on the door that reads: "OUT TO GLUTTONY")*

SIMON: I don't understand. What are you doing?

INTERVIEWER: What does it look like I'm doing? I'm taking one last shot at your soul!

(Music: Hot Jazz—thrilling up tempo)

(The INTERVIEWER puts out his hand. SIMON realizes he must give back his file—his ticket to Heaven...)

(He does...)

(Blackout)

(The music continues, as lights transition to:)

(Happy Hour: The tavern. It is pitch black inside. We hear the first synthesized Karaoke chords of a Disco song [Gloria Gaynor's I Will Survive*].)*

(A spotlight hits the first singer, who happens to be ELVIS PRESLEY *[The Elvis of his later, chunkier Vegas period, replete with white studded jumpsuit].)*

ELVIS: "At first I was afraid—I was petrified!"

(Applause)

ELVIS: Thank you very much. *(Resumes)* "Kept thinking I could never live without you by my side." *(Turns)* Over to you, Franklin.

(Spotlight up on FRANK SINATRA—*again, from the smoky, kooky Vegas years, replete with drink and cigarette.)*

SINATRA: "But then I spent so many nights just feeling sorry for myself—baby this cat grew strong, lemme tell ya, he learned how-to-get-a-long!" *(Turns)* Take it, Fat Boy!

ELVIS: "But now you're back, Moma, from Outer Space—"

SINATRA: Like that outfit of yours—

ELVIS: "I rambled in to find you here with that sad look upon your face."

SINATRA: "I should have changed that stupid lock"

ELVIS: "I should have made you leave your key"

SINATRA: "If I had known for just one second you'd be back annoyin' me!"

ELVIS & SINATRA: "So now go—walk out that door"

ELVIS: "Just turn around now"

SINATRA: "Cuz you ain't welcome anymore (you dirty rat)!"

(On "break me with goodbyes" ELVIS *breaks a board with his dazzling karate prowess:)*

ELVIS: "Weren't you the one who tried to break me with goodbyes? Did you think I'd crumble? Did you think I'd lay down and die?"

*(*SINATRA, *possessed with the power of karoke, lurches into the end of "My Way," as they sing counterpoint to each other.)*

SINATRA: "The record shows—"

ELVIS: *(Continuing "Survive")* "Oh no, not I—"

SINATRA: "I took the blows!"

ELVIS: "I will survive!"

SINATRA: "And did it..."

ELVIS & SINATRA: "MYYYYY WAAAAAAY!"

(The song crescendos, and the lights fade up on the tavern revealing the applauding barflys, who are arranged around two small cocktail tables. A dark mysterious Eastern-European man sits at one table, clothed in a dark cape. A Victorian American woman whistles from behind the bar, a barkeep's towel at her hip.)

(ELVIS and SINATRA make their glorious exit.)

(The INTERVIEWER and SIMON applaud from the corner—SIMON sufficiently impressed.)

SIMON: Wow—Karaoke...in Hell!

INTERVIEWER: Oh Simon—don't tell me you're surprised to see that. *(He starts off.)*

SIMON: Wait—where are you going?

INTERVIEWER: It's Friday night—I never miss an Andy Kaufman concert. Relax, Simon. Mingle. I'll be right back, and when I do, I'll bring a very important person—you may be quite surprised.

SIMON: *(Intrigued)* The Big Boss, right?

(The INTERVIEWER winks. Exits. SIMON looks around, unsure of his next step.)

(He approaches the Barmaid.)

SIMON: Hi. I'm Simon.

(She frowns and turns away.)

(SIMON shrugs and crosses to the man.)

SIMON: Hi. I'm Simon.

(The man looks up.)

EUROPEAN MAN: I'm unimpressed.

(Silence)

SIMON: Can I buy you a drink?

(The man, VLAD THE IMPALER, dressed more like Bela Lugosi, locks eyes with SIMON. He speaks in a thick Carpathian accent.)

VLAD: I do not drink… Wine.

(The bartender, LIZZIE BORDEN calls to VLAD in a thick New England—Boston accent.)

LIZZIE: Oh, give me a break, Bat Boy! *"I do not drink…wine."* You never even *said* that! That was… what's his name… The guy who won the racquetball tournament—

SIMON: Bela Lugosi?

LIZZIE: Right.

VLAD: Don't call me Bat Boy—

SIMON: Bela Lugosi's here?

VLAD: I hate that—

SIMON: *(Crossing to her)* I love Bela Lugosi!

LIZZIE: Vlad and Bela are always fighting—

VLAD: That is a filthy vulgar lie!

LIZZIE: You see, Bela has convinced himself that he is Vlad Dracula, and Vlad has convinced himself that he is Bela Lugosi. Bela sleeps in a coffin. Vlad sleeps in that bottle.

(VLAD puts his arms around his bottle of alcohol, protectively.)

VLAD: Stay away from my bottle. And you are one to talk, Miss Lizzie Borden! I heard you shower with that ax.

(LIZZIE *whips out a huge axe, cradling it.*)

LIZZIE: It's such an awful habit, I know, but it's so comforting to me.

SIMON: *(Backing away)* Of course. Why wouldn't it be?

VLAD: Women. They are so crazy. Lizzie with her ax, Joan with her sword, Eve and her apple—that amazes me. Have you *seen* that apple? It's eight-hundred-thousand years old. She takes it everywhere! "Get a new apple," I tell her, but no—she likes that *particular* apple.

(VLAD *pours himself a drink and gestures for* SIMON *to sit.*)

VLAD: So…?

SIMON: Simon.

VLAD: "Simon?" What did you do?

SIMON: Do…?

VLAD: To get into Hell!

SIMON: But I'm not *in* Hell. I'm just visiting. Really. In fact, to be perfectly honest—

VLAD: Angels and Ministers of Hell defend us!

SIMON: —I'm leaning towards Heaven.

(The others laugh.)

SIMON: Why is that funny?

LIZZIE: Lean wherever you want—you're not going *anywhere*.

SIMON: What do you mean? I told you, I haven't decided yet.

LIZZIE: Well, apparently, someone decided *for* you.

SIMON: *What?*

VLAD: This is going to be the longest six trillion years of your life!

(They are all roaring now.)

SIMON: No…that guy I came in with…his name was…
he looked like… Well you saw him, didn't you?

VLAD: Who?

SIMON: The guy! The guy I came in with!

VLAD: I didn't see anyone.

SIMON: He was just here!

(VLAD shrugs.)

SIMON: No, this is impossible— *(Calling out the door)*
Mister…oh Hell! What's his damn name?

LIZZIE: Do you actually expect us to believe that you
slipped into Hell without the slightest reason as to why
you're here?

SIMON: I don't care what you believe! I just lost my soul
to a Used Car Salesman.

VLAD: That's possible—there are quite a few of them
around here. Only the crooked ones, of course—the
honest ones all go to Heaven.

SIMON: I didn't know there *were* any honest ones.

LIZZIE: There are—thirteen of them.

VLAD: They all worked for Saturn.

Lizzie puts down her work.

LIZZIE: Ok, I give up. How did you, and by you I mean
"you of all people" —slip past the Interview without
knowing it?

SIMON: Don't look at me—I'm as confused as you are…
unless I somehow kvetched myself in here without
realizing it.

VLAD: That's impossible. You must have done
something. The Interview is immune to kvetching. Two
Jews sat on the Drafting Committee.

SIMON: Two Jews? What were two Jews doing in charge of anything? Where were their *wives*?

VLAD: Oh, you'll find the Jews quite assertive here. Tough too. They're constantly beating up Hitler. Without the slightest provocation. He runs around, terrified. They were so docile on Earth, but in Hell, they run around like they *built* the place.

(Spanish music. DON JUAN enters. He is a well dressed Spanish nobleman from the Eighteenth Century, with a thick Castilian accent.)

(LIZZIE stares, thunderstruck.)

LIZZIE: *(Horribly accented)* Buenas Dias.

DON JUAN: *(Uncomfortably)* Buenas Dias, Señora.

(DON JUAN sits at a table and LIZZIE immediately hops over the bar, dramatically draping herself against a chair beside him.)

SIMON: *(Whispering to VLAD)* Hey—who's the stiff collar?

VLAD: Don Juan Tenorio.

SIMON: Don Juan? *The* Don Juan?

VLAD: What other Don Juan is there? Watch this, he's so sensitive. *(Calling over)* Hey, Juan! You gonna kiss her, or what?

DON JUAN: Oh, why don't you leave me alone, already?

LIZZIE: Don't listen to him, Juannie—he's just jealous.

VLAD: Jealous?

DON JUAN: Don't call me Juannie!

She slides down next to him, leaning close.

LIZZIE: Why not me, Juannie?

VLAD: *(Giggling to SIMON)* Here we go...

LIZZIE: Why not me?

VLAD: I love this so much.

(DON JUAN *is now visibly perspiring, as* LIZZIE *moves in.*)

LIZZIE: Why not *me*, Juannie? You've been with that bitch Catherine the Great. What—you fascinated by the Horse thing? Big deal! So she did it with Mister Ed— that's a turn on for you?

DON JUAN: *What?*

LIZZIE: You are sick, mister! You are one sick Spaniard, you know that? Maybe I don't want you. What do you think of that? Maybe you're yesterday's dish— everyone takes a bite, and what's left...isn't worth the digestive effort. *(Beat)* Who am I kidding? Let's go find an empty room and do things I'm going to tell my friends we did anyway.

DON JUAN: Oh, for the love of Lucifer! Why don't you women leave me alone! *(He stands, ripping himself from* LIZZIE'*s grasp. Turns to* SIMON.*)* I heard what you were saying earlier, as I came in. I apologize, I know it was rude to listen, but what you were saying... it was so funny. You think yourself a kvetcher, a great liar, eh?

SIMON: Well, not to toot my own horn, but—

DON JUAN: You are nothing! Nada! You are the whitest lie, the truest false, the shortest tall tale...the anti-fib! You call yourself a liar? Fall to your knees, my friend, you have just met your Patron Saint!

SIMON: Oh, I know. The Women, the Conquests— it's all hyperbole. You haven't slept with *that* many women. I mean, it's impossible...it *has* to be. I hope.

VLAD: He hasn't slept with any.

SIMON: What?

DON JUAN: *(With great pride)* I'm a virgin.

SIMON: *What?*

DON JUAN: What's the matter—I'm speaking Spanish?
I'm a virgin.

SIMON: Don Juan…a virgin?

DON JUAN: Why not? Mary was a virgin, why not me?

SIMON: Well…the stories…the legend—

DON JUAN: Is it so difficult to understand? Not
everyone is in love with sex. It's not that I didn't give it
a try, I did.

*(Lights shift, as LIZZIE becomes Donna Anna, dancing
through embrace after embrace with DON JUAN as he relives
his first Grand Adventure:)*

DON JUAN: One fateful evening, I found myself in the
clutches of Donna Anna de Ulloa, without my clothes,
in an uncomfortable compromising position, when all
of a sudden, the most powerful feeling came over me…
boredom. There I was, in the vise—grip of this saber—
toothed Senora, and I couldn't stop thinking about
this terrific new bean dip recipe I wanted to get from
her—although she was an annoying lover, she had
quite a flair for bean dip. Sensing I was not entirely on
the same page of the Kama Sutra, she demanded that I
ravish her properly. I replied that I was not interested.
She begged! She demanded! She cajoled!

SIMON: So what did you do?

DON JUAN: What do you think I did? I *lied*! I told her
I had been with women, many women, too many
women to count, and that I did not wish to dishonor
her by merely adding her name to that rather lengthy
list. However…if she would be so good as to reveal
that enigmatic bean dip recipe, she was welcome to tell
her friends whatever she wished.

*(DON JUAN suavely spins Donna Anna away, as she fades
back into a disappointed LIZZIE.)*

SIMON: Why didn't you just tell someone the truth?

DON JUAN: *What* truth, eh? The truth is what *is*, correct? Well, I *make* truth. I make it when I relate my conquests to some wide eyed woman, and I make it when I send that woman home to add luster to my legend. The line between true and false is a thin one, my friend, but it takes a *master* to cross that line over and over again until that line no longer *exists*.

(Music: "Girl from Impanema." A young, FASHIONABLE WOMAN, *looking very much like the young Sophia Loren, replete with black dress and dark sunglasses enters. Every head turns and follows her elegant gait across the bar.)*

VLAD: Madam.

*(*FASHIONABLE WOMAN *takes a drink from* VLAD's *offered glass. She then turns to* DON JUAN, *who removes her glasses.)*

DON JUAN: *Señora.*

FASHIONABLE WOMAN: *Signori. (She floats over to a seat at an open table.)*

SIMON: *(Taken)* You know, Hell is really starting to grow on me.

DON JUAN: Give it up, Ackerman. Her heart is not her own.

SIMON: Neither is mine.

*(*SIMON *moves across the bar as suavely as he can as the music fades out.)*

SIMON: If you were to estimate my chances with you on a scale of one to ten, with ten being a very good chance and one being no chance in, well, here—

FASHIONABLE WOMAN: One.

VLAD: Jesus Christ!

(SIMON *turns to* VLAD, *who has stopped cursing and is just staring at him now. He turns back to the* FASHIONABLE WOMAN.)

SIMON: What if I told you I am fully prepared to spend the rest of eternity lubricating your eyelids after their every blink?

FASHIONABLE WOMAN: One half of one.

VLAD: *(Louder)* Jesus Christ!

Simon turns again. Vlad stares back.

SIMON: *(Back to her)* Could I just stalk you for a while? No violence, of course, just the occasional riffling through your underwear drawer?

VLAD: Jesus Christ!

SIMON: *(Spinning back)* What *is* it with you?

VLAD: Jesus Christ. She's got a thing for Jesus Christ.

SIMON: You have a "thing" for Jesus Christ?

FASHIONABLE WOMAN: I better. I'm *married* to him.

SIMON: My God! Jesus Christ—married!

FASHIONABLE WOMAN: Oh no—not exactly.

SIMON: You just said you were married to him.

FASHIONABLE WOMAN: I am.

SIMON: But he's not married to *you.*

FASHIONABLE WOMAN: No.

(SIMON *finally makes the connection.*)

SIMON: You're a nun!

(*The room cheers, half facetiously.*)

SIMON: You don't look like a nun.

FASHIONABLE WOMAN: Neither do you.

SIMON: I'm not a nun.

FASHIONABLE WOMAN: I won't hold it against you, Mister. Uh...

SIMON: *(Overwhelmed)* Schmackerman—Ackerman. Simon Ackerman.

FASHIONABLE WOMAN: *(Offering her hand)* Mother Maria Teresa.

SIMON: *(Shocked)* You're Mother Teresa?

MARIA TERESA: I certainly hope so—I've been telling everyone else I am.

SIMON: Now, hold on a second! This can't be right. I understand, you know, the great liars—

DON JUAN: The Greatest—

SIMON: -and patricidal maniacs—

LIZZIE: How kind of you.

SIMON: —and...whatever the hell *you* are—

VLAD: *(Touched)* Flatterer.

SIMON: —but Mother Teresa? Didn't you feed, like, half the planet?

MARIA TERESA: Yes. And I blackmailed half the Cosa Nostra to pay for it!

(Cheers)

SIMON: I hate to point out the obvious, miss, but when you look like Sophia Loren, you don't have to extort. You can always, just, you know, *ask*.

MARIA TERESA: *(She laughs.)* I didn't always look like her. But I always *felt* like her. And now that I'm here, I can look anyway I please—and this pleases me.

SIMON: Me, too.

VLAD: And how.

DON JUAN: Ay Carumba.

SIMON: *(Beat)* Hey, wait a minute—aren't you still *alive?*

*(*DON JUAN *and* VLAD *stiffen.)*

MARIA TERESA: Circumstances would suggest otherwise.

SIMON: But I—I would have *heard* about it, right?

*(*MARIA TERESA *tenses. From the corner,* DON JUAN *and* VLAD *desperately warn* SIMON.*)*

DON JUAN: Simon—

SIMON: It would have made the news, surely—

VLAD: Mister Ackerman—

SIMON: It would have been everywhere—

DON JUAN: Hey, Kvetchmeister!

*(*SIMON *turns.* DON JUAN *speaks Pig Latin, in his last attempt to warn* SIMON *of impending doom.)*

DON JUAN: Ixnay hetway ethday alktay!

SIMON: No hablay Spaniol, amigo.

DON JUAN: *(Giving up)* Vaya con Dios then, buddy.

SIMON: So, you're dead, eh? Funny—why didn't I hear about it?

MARIA TERESA: There was alot going on that week.

SIMON: *(Eureka!)* Say! Wasn't that the week Princess Dianna died?

MARIA TERESA: *(Exploding)* VENDETTA! *(She whips a stiletto out if her pocket. She hurls* SIMON *onto the table, the knife at his throat.)* Santa Maria, I kill you, you ever speak that name to me again!

SIMON: Princess D—?

DON JUAN & VLAD: NO!

MARIA TERESA: Go ahead, say it. Say it, you receding hairline of a man. SAY IT!

SIMON: I suddenly don't think that's a very good idea.

MARIA TERESA: You don't think I can take it? You don't
think I hear it every second of every minute of every
moment of my afterlife? I was Mother Maria Teresa—
Bharat Ratna, Nobel Prize winner, The Madonna of
Calcutta. Now I "died the same week as Dianna." Or
I didn't. Or who was I in the first place? I've become
the tougher second half of a question on Jeopardy!
(Releases him) If only I'd held a bouncing baby, right?
Silly me—what was I *thinking* feeding millions when
I could have been cuddling babies and speaking out
grandly and wearing wide brimmed hats and holding
benefits at the local Polo grounds? If I had, perhaps I,
too, could have had two and a half *billion* people watch
my funeral. Do you know how many people watched
my funeral in Calcutta? Thirty Seven! Thirty six were
letting the TV run while they ironed their clothes and
the thirty seventh thought he was watching the last
scene in "Gandhi." Do you know there was a thirty-
three percent rise in British suicide the week after her
death? Thirty-three percent! Do you know the suicide
rate in Calcutta the week after I died? ZERO. Want
to know why? BECAUSE I NEVER LET ANYONE
WORSHIP ME! I asked people to eat, do good works,
and find their own way to Heaven. What an *idiot*!
(Sighs) I have nothing against her *personally*. She's
happy up in Heaven with her floppy hats and her
perfect nipples and her Received Pronunciation, and
God bless her. *(Seriously)* But the Magnetic North of
Human Adoration went through a profound polar shift
that day, and I'd blame the press, and I'd blame the
rankest corners of the rank and file whose hysterical
catharses drag the rest of us, Pied Piper like, into a
mindless mass existence as parasitic Pilot Fish, sucking
on the brine shrimp discards of the faintly famous to
avoid gazing into the empty chasm of our own failed

lives; but in the end…I have to blame humanity itself. And that, my friend, to someone who spent her entire life fighting for the preservation of it…that hurts. *(She tosses aside the stiletto in disgust and collapses back into her seat.)*

(SIMON stares at MARIA TERESA, absolutely floored.)

SIMON: *(Genuinely)* Well I don't think that's *right.*

MARIA TERESA: *(Pause)* O K, then—you can stay.

SIMON: Hold on, I'm not exactly sure I want to.

MARIA TERESA: Fine. Go to Heaven. Buy a Dianna shirt. You'll love it. *(She crosses to the bar for a drink.)*

(DON JUAN crosses to SIMON, intrigued.)

DON JUAN: This just doesn't add up, Senor Acerkman—your being here and being, well…

SIMON: Me?

DON JUAN: Yes. How exactly did you come to be "Organically Impaired"?

SIMON: You mean how did I die?

DON JUAN: We like to say:

ALL: "Organically Impaired."

SIMON: *(Humiliated)* Sushi.

(They burst out laughing.)

DON JUAN: You were eaten by an angry flounder?

SIMON: No—

DON JUAN: What a way to go!

SIMON: No. I just ate one Hamachi too many. That's the last thing I remember. My wife , she says, "Don't get the Hamachi, you always get the Hamachi!" And I said "I like the Hamachi," which is true, I like the Hamachi, always have, and she says "That's it! I hate you, I hate the Hamachi, and I hope you choke on it!" Two hours later, I'm looking up from the emergency room bed at this fading figure of my wife. She's *smiling* for, I believe, the first time in her entire life, and she says "Schmuck! I told you not to get the Hamachi!" Next thing I know, I'm sitting across from this self important civil servant who smiles alot and reeks of Jovan Musk. Apparently he liked me, because next thing I know, he drags me here and tells me to wait for some bozo.

(The four of them all share a look.)

MARIA TERESA: Some *bozo*?

SIMON: Yeah. He didn't tell me his name. I'm supposed to recognize him, or he's supposed to recognize me, or something like that.

DON JUAN: *(Looking to the others)* Well, my friends, it appears we have a celebrity in our midst.

SIMON: *(Blushing)* Get outta here!

DON JUAN: A celebrity I tell you…when no less a figure than *Lucifer* himself is coming to greet you.

(DON JUAN *moves off to sit with the others, leaving* SIMON *alone.)*

SIMON: Lucifer?

LIZZIE: The Son of Morning.

MARIA TERESA: In the flesh.

VLAD: *(Simmering)* You lucky bastard.

SIMON: Lucifer? You're crazy. Why the devil would Lucifer want to meet me? I'm the one who put the schmuck in schmoe.

(VLAD *leaps up, bursting out:)*

VLAD: This is an outrage!

Don Juan moves to calm Vlad.

DON JUAN: Vlad—easy—

VLAD: Don't touch me, "Celibate Charlie!"

LIZZIE: Vlad—

VLAD: *(Menacing* SIMON*)* Who are *you?*

*(*MARIA TERESA *moves to him.)*

MARIA TERESA: Vlad—

VLAD: *(Throwing her off)* Who are you?!

SIMON: I'm Simon—

VLAD: *Simon* who? Simon the Great? Simon the
Destroyer? Simon the Terrible? Or are you Simon
the *Accountant?* Simon the Not So Great? Simon the
Terrified? I'm Vlad the Impaler! Who are you? Who are
you, that Lucifer himself should greet you and not me?
Now I don't pretend to be as famous or as infamous as
Don Juan—

DON JUAN: *(Mournfully)* He didn't greet me either—

VLAD: But, well, being the world's first mass murderer,
I'm relatively well known—

LIZZIE: Bela's well known—

VLAD: Forget Bela! When I came to Hell, the name
Dracula meant a great deal more than long pointy
teeth and an inaccurate Moldavian accent. I was Vlad
Tepes—Vlad the Impaler, ten times more ruthless than
that foppish celluloid *bat* that bears my name. And yet,
for all my protestation, I will forever be confused with
Bram Stoker's buck toothed perversion for all eternity.

SIMON: But the blood…?

VLAD: That is such a myth!

SIMON: That you drank blood?

VLAD: No, that I *enjoyed* drinking blood. Sometimes one
must do things for an effect. Panache, you understand.
In the fifteenth century, genocide had become terribly
generic. Everyone was doing it. Of course the *Crusaders*

were the worst offenders of the bunch—leave it to the
Church to find a way to make mass murder for mass
consumption. When they killed, they did it in "God's
name," and for some reason, that made murder a
sacrament, and not a sin. Now I ask you: WHERE'S
THE FUN IN THAT!? When you take the sin out of
murder, you take the *sex* out of sin. In their misguided
religious fervor, they were unable to see that they
were tinkering with an *art form* that has been around
since Cain looked at Abel, and saw that a blow to the
head might actually make his brother's appearance
more aesthetically pleasing. *(Desperately)* I needed an
angle, you see. A fresh approach. Now, one afternoon,
during a somewhat raunchy torture session, this ill-
mannered fool began bleeding all over my dinner,
squirting his life into my wine glass, without a thought
in the world as to the terribly awkward position it
was putting me in. Everyone in the court was looking.
What was I supposed to *do*? *(He gazes into an imaginary
wine glass and gulps it down.)* At first, it turned out
to be just the thing—news spread quickly of the
"Ruthless Blood Drinking Prince Vlad." Unfortunately,
after a time, it became all the rage. So, what now?
Back to Beheadings? Boiling the flesh? Hanging?
Disemboweling—they had all lost their luster. Then,
when I was at the apogee of my unhappiness, I had
the most wonderful vision... *Impalement.* Now I was
confident, but not hubristically so—the Church had
stolen my thunder before. I waited on word from
Rome with bated breath. Finally, the Pope released
an encyclical, stating quite clearly his, and therefore
God's, opposition to impalement. He declared, and I'm
paraphrasing here, that "No pole should go where not
even God *himself* had license to go!" My triumph over
the mighty forces of mediocrity was undeniable and
complete. The moment that first pole crept up that first
colon, I became for all eternity: "Vlad the Impaler-"

godless, soulless, merciless…but an unequivocal *original!*

(SIMON *stares, awe-struck.*)

SIMON: And after all that, and I must say that it's all quite impressive, but after all that, Lucifer didn't welcome you in person?

VLAD: *(Mournfully)* No. He didn't. I received a "Welcome to Hell" hallmark card from his office with a photocopied letter and a reproduced signature.

LIZZIE: You got a card? Argh! You men and your exclusive clubs! All I got was a T-shirt. It said "I got sent to Hell, and all they gave me was this lousy T-shirt."

SIMON: I'm sorry. I am. Really. I don't know what to *say.*

VLAD: Don't say anything. Just go. Go now. Go before I find out where Moliere hid all my impalement poles.

SIMON: Go? Where?

VLAD: Go back to where you belong. Go to Heaven.

SIMON: Now wait a minute—I'm not so sure anymore. This place has its own…kinky sort of charm, you know—and I'm…I'm kind of getting *into* it.

VLAD: Well find a way to get *out* of it.

Lizzie takes Simon by the collar, and begins dragging him towards the front door.

LIZZIE: Goodbye, Simon Ackerman.

SIMON: Wait a sec!

MARIA TERESA: It's been an insincere pleasure.

SIMON: I think we got off on the wrong foot here—

VLAD: You belong up there, all curled up in comfortable conformity—

SIMON: But I thought I had a choice—

VLAD: You do. Now choose Heaven.

(VLAD shoves him to the lip of the exit.)

DON JUAN: Goodbye Mister Accountant.

SIMON: *(Throwing them off)* Now hold on, I won't stand for that. You can call me many things— "Accountant" is not one of them.

LIZZIE: *(Snickering)* So, what were you, Simon? An *Assassin*? An Anarchist, perhaps?

SIMON: *(Proudly)* A *Lawyer*, actually.

(DON JUAN, MARIA TERESA and VLAD burst out laughing.)

(LIZZIE, stunned instead, bends over the table.)

SIMON: What's so funny?

(They laugh harder.)

SIMON: What's so damn funny about being a lawyer?

(They are in tears now.)

DON JUAN, MARIA & VLAD: All lawyers go to Heaven!

(DON JUAN and VLAD fall to the floor in hysterics.)

(Unbeknownst to all, LIZZIE has picked up her ax. Without a sound, she takes a swing at SIMON, which only serves to send the others into deeper hysterics.)

LIZZIE: I...HATE...LAWYERS!

DON JUAN: *(Through tears)* Senora Borden has a slight aversion to lawyers.

SIMON: Thanks for the heads up, Juan.

(LIZZIE takes another swing with the ax.)

LIZZIE: I...HATE...LAWYERS! *(She hurls SIMON onto the table, holding the ax at his throat.)* They wouldn't let me testify! The bastards wouldn't let me testify.

So I got off. "Not Guilty." How *humiliating*. Every
one in town— "Did she do it?"... "I don't know." ...
"Maybe." *Maybe?* Hacked my parents into mincemeat,
and *that* will be my legacy. MAYBE! My one great
act of self expression, diluted in a wash of innocuous
legality. *(She releases* SIMON *and goes to get a drink.)* And
let me tell you something—I did not go through all that
so I could spend eternity...with a lawyer. *(She spits on
the floor and walks off.)*

*(*DON JUAN *and* VLAD *have arisen, but remain snickering.*
MARIA TERESA *dabs her eyes.)*

MARIA TERESA: I think I burst a capillary.

DON JUAN: Someone really screwed the pooch with
you, my friend.

VLAD: That's the funniest thing I've heard in four
hundred years! All lawyers go to Heaven!

SIMON: What are you talking about? There must be
Lawyers in Hell. Lawyers are ruthless cash crazed
opportunists.

VLAD: Precisely. Where's the originality in that?
Objections—

DON JUAN: Procedure—

MARIA TERESA: Habeas Corpus—

VLAD: It's all *Precedent*, right?

SIMON: Well...

VLAD: You do what was done before, yes? That's the
very *definition* of Heaven. We're not punishing you—
we're *protecting* you from an eternity of agony. Go to
Heaven.

LIZZIE: Enough of this! At first it was amusing, but all
this conformity is starting to make me nauseous.

MARIA TERESA: This is Hell, for crying out loud! Have they no decency? Accepting Lawyers? What's next— Theatrical Agents?

DON JUAN: I have a friend in Immigration. There must be something we can do.

(They go for the exit.)

SIMON: WAIT!

(Something in SIMON's voice stops them.)

SIMON: *(Dejectedly)* Wait. You don't have to do that. I'll go.

(DON JUAN puts his arm around SIMON and walks him toward the door.)

DON JUAN: Don't be so glum, Simon. This is for the best, believe me. You just don't *fit.* One piece of advice, though—when you get to Heaven, resist the temptation to join a choir. No one up there has a clue about music. They haven't picked up a decent musician in the last hundred years, and they're not due for another until Yanni dies.

(The INTERVIEWER bursts through the door, laughing.)

INTERVIEWER: That Andy Kaufman is a *riot!* You know how he likes to wrestle women, right? Well he brought up one of the Sabine Women tonight, and she kicked the shit out of him! Now *that's* Comedy! *(He spots Simon going to Heaven. Goes after him)* Well, hello there, Simon. Where are you off to?

SIMON: Heaven.

INTERVIEWER: *Heaven?* God forbid! Why?

SIMON: I don't belong here.

INTERVIEWER: Oh that's silly. Who put that funny idea into your head?

LIZZIE: We did.

DON JUAN: We certainly did. Who the hell are you?

VLAD: I know this guy. He looks terribly familiar. I can't place the face.

INTERVIEWER: That's because this *isn't* my face. I change it from time to time— Variety: the spice of the afterlife!

MARIA TERESA: He did my interview.

VLAD: That's right! He did mine too.

INTERVIEWER: Yes I believe I had the distinct pleasure of interviewing all of you. Especially our illustrious Mister Ackerman here.

VLAD: Simon? You've got to be kidding.

INTERVIEWER: Did he tell you why he's here?

SIMON: How could I tell them why I'm here? I don't have the slightest idea!

INTERVIEWER: Of course you don't, silly… *(He brandishes a file. Smiles.)* But I do.

(God's music blasts into the scene.)

INTERVIEWER: Well! It's about time!

SIMON: What? Is that…? The Big Boss?

INTERVIEWER: Right on schedule—late.

MARIA TERESA: Wait— That's not…

DON JUAN: It couldn't be…

LIZZIE: It is.

INTERVIEWER: God.

SIMON: God? … "GOD" God?

INTERVIEWER: One's enough, Simon, believe me.

VLAD: Well—there goes the Underworld!

(GABRIEL and GOD enter. GOD points majestically at the INTERVIEWER.)

GOD: Avaunt, thou Demon! Take your hands off that sweet child of Heaven!

(*Crack of thunder.* SIMON *is invisibly pulled to* GOD's *side.*)

GABRIEL: Astonishing, My Lord. The way that wayward sheep returned to the fold so quickly.

GOD: Shut up, Gabriel.

INTERVIEWER: Shouldn't you be off somewhere creating brave new worlds?

GOD: You know very well I'm tired of all that crap. I've burned my last bush, my friend.

(GOD *collapses into the nearest chair. The* INTERVIEWER *brings her a drink.*)

INTERVIEWER: What happened? You were the Greatest Show on Earth for five billion years running! The Creation, The Flood, The Eight Nights of Miraculous Candlelight—

GOD: Hey, cut me some slack on Hanukkah, okay— they can't *all* be show stoppers.

INTERVIEWER: So what Happened?

GOD: I tell you, that damned Renaissance completely wore me out. Thirty Two Thousand Earthly manifestations, just to have that hack Michelangelo and every two bit prick with a paintbrush give me a beard, a bad haircut, and a receding hairline. And all those *zaftig* Pre-Raphaelites flapping their udders across every canvas in Europe. Everyone gets a boob but me, for crying out load! No, I'm retired. Finished. I've taken a cloud over to Miami and sneak onto the golf course every now and then.

INTERVIEWER: How's your game?

GABRIEL: It's wonderful!

GOD: It's passable.

INTERVIEWER: You still cheat?

GOD: I had nothing to do with that breeze on the thirteenth hole, and you know it!

INTERVIEWER: It wasn't the breeze I was referring to. It was the tornado in the sand trap.

GOD: Oh...well, I might have had something to do with *that*. So, imagine my surprise, my friend, when right in the middle of one of my best games in centuries—it was a good game, wasn't it, Gabriel?

GABRIEL: Superlative, My Lord!

GOD: I had to ask. Well, as I was saying, imagine my surprise when, on the final putt, my celestial cellular rings to tell me you're stealing one of my souls.

INTERVIEWER: One of *your* souls!

GOD: One of my most precious ones. His whole life has been a model of obedience. A paragon of consistency.

INTERVIEWER: Not exactly. According to this— *(Brandishes file)* —he was taken, mistakenly I might add, the night before what might have been his Defining Moment.

GOD: *(Non-chalantly)* Oh, this is *that* one, eh?

INTERVIEWER: Yes, this is *that* one.

SIMON: What one? Which one am I?

INTERVIEWER: Well Simon, you said before you didn't do anything, anything interesting, and you were right. You didn't get the chance. You see, we sort of made a little...Boo-Boo with you.

SIMON: A "Boo Boo?"

INTERVIEWER: Just a little one. You see, every soul on Earth gets at least one, what we like to call, *Defining Moment*—that moment when you are presented with a clear choice—Heaven or Hell. You had one, well you

were *scheduled* to have one, but apparently, you were...
well—*taken* the night before you could have it!

SIMON: *What?*

INTERVIEWER: Exactly. Remember that fateful Hamachi?

SIMON: You mean, the one that made me...

ALL: Organically Impaired.

INTERVIEWER: Yes. Well, it was in actuality, and listen
very carefully to this, your *Wife* whose time was up,
but apparently, she inadvertently switched her iodine
infested halibut with your hamachi the night before
what should have been your Defining Moment! At
least, that's what it says *here*, under this scribbled out
section...

(Before he can look any closer, GODswipes the file.)

GOD: Defining moment my ass! His whole *life* was
filled with Defining Moments. *(Reads the file)* Never
spent a single moment in the Principal's office. Never
talked back to his parents. Never late for work, never
worked late. Never grumbled at either the length of the
Academy Awards nor the choice of the winners. Never
saw movies until after they had been reviewed, and
only then if they had been *well* reviewed. Wore Izod
shirts, 501's, Dockers, drank Coke when it was "The
Real Thing," and Pepsi when it was "The Choice of a
New Generation," etc, etc, etc!

LIZZIE: Oh, Simon—Izod Shirts?!?! Just tell me you
didn't turn the collar up.

(SIMON shrugs.)

INTERVIEWER: Izod aside, all this is meaningless. Simon
was on the threshold of throwing off the trappings
of conformity to take his rightful place among the
Demons.

GOD: You cannot assume you have any idea he would do anything differently.

INTERVIEWER: And you cannot assume he would continue to act like such a Yentz!

(GOD *and the* INTERVIEWER *face off.*)

GOD: Very well. We settle this. The Ancient Way.

INTERVIEWER: The Ancient Way it is.

ALL: *(Chanting)* The Ancient Way, The Ancient Way, They're doing it the Ancient Way!

(GOD *and the* INTERVIEWER *move into the center of the room and prepare to duel. Both raise a clenched fist, and at the same time…*)

GOD & INTERVIEWER: Rock, paper, scissors…

SIMON: *What* are you doing?

GOD: This is the way we do it.

SIMON: The way you do *what*?

INTERVIEWER: The way we settle things.

SIMON: You play "Rock Paper Scissors"?

INTERVIEWER: You know a better way?

SIMON: You can't play "Rock Paper Scissors" for my soul!

GOD: Why not? What makes you so special?

SIMON: *(Exploding)* I will *not* have my eternity determined by which one of you chooses "paper!"

GOD: I always choose scissors—

SIMON: Let it go, God. Just—let it go. *(Takes a deep breath)* Now, at the risk of offending the Almighty, and the… All-Lowly, I respectfully ask that you stop your incessant squabbling and figure out some sensible way to resolve this.

INTERVIEWER: Don't think too harshly of us, Simon. We're only Gods, you know—we can't be expected to do *everything* right.

GOD: Speak for yourself, my friend! I always have a plan, even if it appears, on the surface, to have the thin veneer of Chaos.

SIMON: Well, I think I'm choking on your veneer, here.

INTERVIEWER: Then perhaps we can offer you a Heavenly Heimlich!

GOD: How so?

INTERVIEWER: Well, we do appear to have come upon an *obstruction*, as Simon so elegantly put it. Our mistake—

(GOD *clears her throat.*)

INTERVIEWER: Our finely honed plan—unfortunately placed Simon in the unenviable position that he was unable to choose. His Universal Right to a Defining Moment was denied him!

GOD: That's not *my* fault! As I said: I am very, very, *very* sorry.

INTERVIEWER: Well, if, as you say, you are feeling particularly contrite, you could always, you know… remove the obstruction.

GOD: What obstruction?

INTERVIEWER: Let him go *through* with it.

GOD: Through with what?

SIMON: Of *course*! I have to go *through* with it!

WHOLE BAR He has to go through with it!

GOD: You've lost me. Back up. Through with what?

SIMON: I have to have my Defining Moment! Make my choice. Then we'll know where I truly belong.

GOD: *(Beat)* I don't think that's a very good idea at all.

INTERVIEWER: I think it's a marvellous idea!

GOD: You're wasting your time, my friend. Look at him—he's dead! "Rules are Rules." We judge them by their life on Earth. Period. Not what their life *might* have been.

INTERVIEWER: Ah! I see. I suppose we must play by the *rules*, then, must we?

GOD: We *all* must. The balance of the Universe depends on it.

INTERVIEWER: Very well, then, my Lord, you win. And bravo to you, well played! *But*, just for the Hell of it—

(GOD grumbles.)

INTERVIEWER: Or for the Heaven of it, for that matter.

(Barflys grumble.)

INTERVIEWER: Just for the *drama* of it all, why don't you let him *try* it anyway.

GOD: *(Skeptically)* Why does it matter to you?

SIMON: It matters to *me*.

(The strength of this brings silence.)

SIMON: I want to know. Even if it has no bearing whatsoever. I want to know.

VLAD: So do I.

DON JUAN: Me too.

MARIA TERESA: I can't help it.

LIZZIE: You guys are nuts.

(GOD is visibly wavering, tortured.)

GABRIEL: *(Anxiously)* My Lord…?

SIMON: Please God—I've never asked you for anything before.

GOD: That's not true. You asked to get laid on Prom Night.

SIMON: You heard that?

GOD: How the hell do you think it happened?

GABRIEL: My Lord?

INTERVIEWER: Bad form denying a Last Request, you know.

GOD: Oy—a *Last Request*?

GABRIEL: *(Insistently)* My Lord?!

GOD: What *is* it, Gabriel?

GABRIEL: *(Hinting as best he can)* Don't you need to... you know—

GOD: What?

GABRIEL: Go?

GOD: Go *where*?

GABRIEL: That place you wanted to go— Near the other place— Across from the You Know.

GOD: ARE YOU TRYING TO GIVE ME AN ANEURYSM?

INTERVIEWER: His *Last Request*, my Lord...

GOD: *(Bursting out)* Very well. I'll be damned if I'm going to let it get around that I denied a Last Request. *(To* INTERVIEWER*)* I don't know what you're up to, but you be careful with this.

*(*INTERVIEWER *nods.* GOD *retreats.)*

(The INTERVIEWER *snaps his fingers. Lights down on him as the others set up the "Courtroom", which clearly resembles the Heavenly courtroom of "The Trial". When the Trial eventually begins, Lights will track* GOD *and the* INTERVIEWER *as they watch the action unfold.)*

(The INTERVIEWER *puts his arm around* SIMON *and walks him into the middle of the room.)*

INTERVIEWER: Now Simon, once we begin, you'll be back. In your life on Earth, as it was—although you might find yourself slightly altered from your adventures here. Or perhaps you won't. The choice, of course, is yours. *(He places his hands over* SIMON*'s eyes.)* Now, think back Simon. You died the night before… what?

SIMON: *That* was to be my defining moment? It was just a run of the mill date rape defense. It was just another trial.

INTERVIEWER: That, Simon, depends on you.

*(*INTERVIEWER *snaps his fingers. Lights change.)*

(The PROSECUTOR *[actor who plays* GABRIEL*] bursts past Simon— we are now in the* JUDGE*'s chambers [actor who plays* VLAD*]. The* PROSECUTOR *brandishes a white purse.)*

PROSECUTOR: You can't let him use this, your Honor!

*(*SIMON *gawks at them, astonished.)*

SIMON: My God— you look so lifelike!

JUDGE: I appreciate the compliment, Mister Ackerman, but what precisely does that have to do with the alleged victim's purse, and more to the point, why on Earth I should allow it in my courtroom?

SIMON: Purse? *(Notices purse)* Oh, *that* purse! *(Feeling his way back)* Well, your Honor— as you know, she surprised the defendant at his house, late at night, wearing next to nothing—

JUDGE: What's in the *purse*, Simon?

*(*SIMON *snatches the purse from the* PROSECUTOR*. Opens it up, and removes a condom.)*

SIMON: Condoms, your Honor. Quite a few of them, actually. "Ribbed, for her pleasure."

PROSECUTOR: *(Grabs purse)* Your Honor. It's irrelevant. It's inflammatory—

JUDGE: It's *showtime*, gentlemen.

(The JUDGE *grabs the purse, and passes it to* SIMON *on his way back to the "Courtroom". The* PROSECUTOR *remains, glaring at* SIMON.*)*

PROSECUTOR: Does it matter to you that he raped her? That you're defending a rapist?

SIMON: I'm not defending him. I'm *representing* him.

PROSECUTOR: Don't delude yourself. You're also representing *you*.

*(*PROSECUTOR *pushes past* SIMON. *Lights shift into the courtroom.)*

(The JUDGE *bangs the gavel. The* VICTIM *sits in the witness stand, the* RAPIST *by* SIMON.*)*

*(*GOD *and* INTERVIEWER *watch, apart)*

JUDGE: Ladies and Gentlemen, I apologize for the delay—Counsel?

SIMON: Thank you, your Honor.

*(*SIMON *addresses the audience, which serve as the jury. He has by now regained his composure—as well as his old attitude…)*

SIMON: Let's get back to the facts, shall we? Now, on the night in question—you remember the night in question, don't you?

VICTIM: Very well.

SIMON: Then I suppose you can tell the court if you remember bringing your *purse* that night.

(SIMON *takes out the white purse and dumps it right in front of the* VICTIM's *nose. She stares at the purse with the realization of what it surely contains.*)

VICTIM: Yes.

SIMON: "Yes", you remember, or "Yes", you brought it?

VICTIM: Yes, I brought it.

SIMON: Good. Then in your purse that night, you had, what? A wallet?

VICTIM: Yes.

SIMON: Keys?

VICTIM: Yes.

SIMON: Anything *else*?

PROSECUTOR: Objection!

JUDGE: Overruled.

SIMON: On the night that you came over to the Defendant's house, the night you came over well past *midnight*, wearing a raincoat—and nothing else I might add—on that night, was there anything *else* in your purse besides your wallet and your keys?

(Silence)

PROSECUTOR: Moment with the witness your honor?

JUDGE: A brief one, Counsel.

(*The* PROSECUTOR *offers the* VICTIM *a tissue to dry her tears while* SIMON *confers confidentially with the* RAPIST.)

RAPIST: You are worth every fucking penny, you know that?

SIMON: Just doing my job.

RAPIST: Well you do your job extremely well, my friend. No wonder they call you "The Man's Man".

SIMON: "The Man's Man"? Who calls me that?

RAPIST: *(As if he should know)* Everyone. You know—
you rape a girl, you call The Man's Man. That's you.
That's what we call you. That's what you *are.*

*(*SIMON *falls silent. The* JUDGE *impatiently clears his
throat.)*

JUDGE: Mister Ackerman—may we continue?

SIMON: *(Snapping out)* Uhm...yes. Sorry. *(He approaches
the* VICTIM.*)* What was I...? We were talking about...
(Notices purse on stand) Your purse, right?

VICTIM: Yes.

SIMON: And you were recalling...you *recalled*
something you had brought with you in that purse, am
I correct?

VICTIM: *(Crying)* Yes.

SIMON: And... Please don't cry.

VICTIM: I'm sorry.

JUDGE: Please continue, Counsel.

SIMON: Yes. Sorry. Now, about those "things" in your
purse... If I asked you to tell the court what those
"things" were...you would *tell* us, wouldn't you?

VICTIM: Yes. If you asked me.

SIMON: *(Beat)* If I *asked* you?

VICTIM: Yes. If you asked me, I would *have* to.

SIMON: *(Realizing)* Yes. I suppose you would. *(He slowly
approaches the* VICTIM *and picks up the purse. Looks at the*
VICTIM's *face. At the* RAPIST. *Stops)*

JUDGE: Counsel?

SIMON: Yes. Sorry, your Honor. Well then, Miss Eve,
you tell me you brought something in your purse that
night, and I just happen to *have* that purse right here,

and so I suppose there is only one thing left for me to say:

(The room holds its breath as SIMON *reaches into the purse... He freezes. He suddenly looks up.)*

SIMON: "No further questions."

(Silence)

JUDGE: Counsel—are you *sure*?

*(*SIMON *removes an empty hand from the purse.)*

SIMON: *(Resolutely)* Yup. No further questions! *(He walks away from the stand.)*

JUDGE: Counsel. Simon! Bethink yourself!

*(*SIMON *drops the purse on the* PROSECUTOR's *table as the* JUDGE *bangs his gavel.)*

JUDGE: Mister Ackerman! Approach the bench! Approach the bench this instant!

*(*SIMON *sits contentedly back down.)*

RAPIST: What the fuck are you doing, man? I paid you good money! You call yourself a lawyer? What do you have to say for yourself?

SIMON: *(Smiling)* No further questions.

(The RAPIST *whips out a concealed knife.)*

RAPIST: No further questions is right!

*(*RAPIST *cuts* SIMON's *throat. All scream.)*

(Crash of thunder)

(Everyone freezes. Time stops. Silence)

*(*GOD *gingerly approaches the* INTERVIEWER.)*

INTERVIEWER: Well. That's a bit of a surprise, isn't it? *(Beat)* Or *is* it?

GOD: This changes nothing, you know. He's mine!

INTERVIEWER: Of course. I wouldn't dream of changing anything, my Lord. "Rules are rules," as you say.

(GOD *snaps her finger. Lights up. Commotion from all— we are back in the present.* SIMON *is alone in the center, grasping at his throat.*)

SIMON: What the hell was that!?

INTERVIEWER: Simon, are you alright?

SIMON: Yes, I'm…I'm…I think.

GOD: Alright, you two have had your fun. Let's go, Simon.

(SIMON *turns to the* INTERVIEWER, *thrilled.*)

SIMON: So, I did it…I really *did* it?

INTERVIEWER: Not bad for a lawyer, eh Simon?

SIMON: Not bad at all.

INTERVIEWER: *(Beat)* Bad luck not getting your shot on Earth, yes?

SIMON: *(Thinking)* Yeah. If only I hadn't eaten that damn Hamachi—

(GOD *suddenly leaps between the* INTERVIEWER *and* SIMON.)

GOD: Well, sorry to gloat and run. Come on, Simon, before I turn you into a Pillar of Saltines.

(GOD *hustles* SIMON *to the door.*)

INTERVIEWER: Simon!

(SIMON *halts*)

INTERVIEWER: *Bad Luck.*

SIMON: Yeah. Bad Luck. *(He slowly exits, this last exchange clearly troubling him…)*

(GOD *gloats.*)

GOD: As I said, my friend: "Adam will be their—"

(SIMON *bursts back in, puzzle solved.*)

SIMON: How could I be so stupid! I'm so sorry my Lord, I never *thanked* you!

GOD: That's true. You didn't. *(Beat)* Thanked me for what?

SIMON: That brutal stabbing. You saved me from it.

GOD: That's true! I did! You see? You all see? I'm not nearly the vengeful God they make me out to be! I knew the pain that lay before you, so I stepped in at the last moment to spare you the misery!

(SIMON *shares a smile with the* INTERVIEWER.)

SIMON: "Stepped in?" I'm sorry, I'm terribly confused. Maybe this is just the *lawyer* in me, but I thought... *(Snatching his file, crossing to* INTERVIEWER*)* Well, you told me my *wife* allegedly switched my Hamachi with her poisoned Halibut when I went to the bathroom.

INTERVIEWER: *(Referring to file)* Well, that's the information I received from my good friend Gabriel over there.

SIMON: Yes, but now it appears it was God *Herself*, who made the fateful switch.

INTERVIEWER: Well that's *funny*.

(The INTERVIEWER *and* SIMON *both turn to* GOD.)

GOD: Now, hold on—I can explain—

SIMON: And not only that, I seem to remember, yes—I *clearly* remember my wife's famous last words.

ALL: "Schmuck! I told you not to get the *Hamachi*!"

SIMON: Now why would she have said *that* if she had *switched* them?

INTERVIEWER: I wonder.

SIMON: *(To* GOD*)* It was *you*, wasn't it? Not my wife. *You* switched them. You *knew* what I would do, so you *took* me before I could do it.

*(*GOD *is silent.)*

SIMON: Well? What do you have to say for yourself?

GOD: *(Sheepishly)* "I am that I am?"

SIMON: Yes. You certainly are.

GOD: Don't be fooled, Simon. Hell has it's share of psychopaths as well as it's share of poets. If you have a drink with Moliere, you must also have one with Mussolini. Choose *one*...choose *all*.

*(*SIMON *stares at* GOD*, uncommitted either way.)*

GOD: Very well, Simon. You win. "Rules are Rules," I suppose. Make your choice. I trust you'll make the wise one... You did all your *Earthly* Life. *(Back to the* INTERVIEWER*)* And as for *you*...keep working on your swing. Next time we play, expect more than a little tornado on the thirteenth hole!

*(*GOD *exits.* GABRIEL *follows. At the exit, he turns back to* SIMON*, full of betrayal.)*

GABRIEL: And you...a *lawyer. (He exits.)*

*(*SIMON *turns back to find the whole room staring over him.)*

LIZZIE: I believe we owe you an apology, Mister Ackerman.

SIMON: *(As cooly as he can)* Save it, kid.

DON JUAN: So, what's the choice, Simon? Where are you going to go?

SIMON: *(Toying with them)* I'm not completely sure. I mean, you all seemed hell bent against my staying here.

(They loudly protest.)

SIMON: Wait a minute—didn't you all just tell me to go to Heaven?

VLAD: *(Giving him a "noogie")* You don't want to go to *Heaven!* All those drooling Cherubs and Haloes...and Republicans!

(SIMON notices the INTERVIEWER sneaking off.)

SIMON: Hey! Where are you going?

INTERVIEWER: Business calls. No rest for the wicked, you know. Goodbye Simon Ackerman. It was a pleasure to meet you.

SIMON: Likewise. *(Whispers)* I think I'll let them convince me to stay.

INTERVIEWER: Good. I think you would be terribly unhappy anywhere else. You see, Simon, when it all comes down to it, Hell is a state of mind. It's a way of looking at life, or the Afterlife for that matter. We don't demand a body count, we don't demand a symphony. We don't prefer Einsteins, or Eisensteins, or Caesars. We just ask for good or bad, for right or wrong, that you do something...*different*. Something that's never been done before. A step no one has taken, a word no one has written, a rule no one has broken. Simple. And yet, not so simple for most.

SIMON: Thank you.

INTERVIEWER: No, Simon. Thank *you*. Your kind cross my desk so infrequently these days. Conformity's greatest sin isn't suppression, Simon, it's *sterilization*. So when I look at *you*, at what one small, seemingly insignificant act of defiance can accomplish, I am, once again, content to await the promise of the future. Farewell.

(WILLIAM SHAKESPEARE bursts in with two scripts.)

WILLIAM SHAKESPEARE: Hey! Which one of you
schmucks is Simon Ackerman?

SIMON: I am. I'm Simon.

(WILLIAM SHAKESPEARE *spots the* INTERVIEWER.)

WILLIAM SHAKESPEARE: Well, hello there, friend! How's
business?

INTERVIEWER: Good Bill, good. Gotta run. *(He turns one
last time to* SIMON.) Take care, Simon. What I wouldn't
give for five billion more like you. Ah well…we must
be content with the trickle, for now—there's a mighty
strong hand on that faucet. Good day. *(He warmly nods
to all as he exits.)*

WILLIAM SHAKESPEARE: What a guy! *(He grabs* SIMON's
hand and shakes it with gusto.) Bill Shakespeare!
Pleasure to meet you, Simon. You're the Toast of the
Underworld!

SIMON: Me? You're kidding. Why?

WILLIAM SHAKESPEARE: "No further questions!" That's
why! That phrase is all the rage. Bartlett put it in his
book. Moses put it in Stone. E. E. Cummings took a
felt tip pen and wrote it on the wall of every bathroom
in Hell—and not only that…he used CAPITALS! Can
you believe it? *(He opens up the first script and points out
something.)* You see here, what I've done? I've amended
my two most famous lines—in your Honor. Read it! Go
ahead!

SIMON: *(Reading)* "The first thing we do, is kill all the
Lawyers…except Simon Ackerman."

WILLIAM SHAKESPEARE: I love it! *(Searching another
script)* And…lets see—this is my favorite—here we
go… "To be, or not to be… No further questions!"

SIMON: Wow.

WILLIAM SHAKESPEARE: Huh? I love it! I love it! You've knocked all Hell on it's *ass*!

(DON JUAN *makes for the bar.*)

DON JUAN: Come on, let's celebrate! This is Hell, you know.

VLAD: Wait! Shouldn't we wait for Lucifer?

WILLIAM SHAKESPEARE: Lucifer? You just missed him.

LIZZIE: What?

MARIA TERESA: What do you mean?

WILLIAM SHAKESPEARE: He was just here. You know—hundred dollar haircut, Buster Brown shoes, Jovan Musk…that's Lucifer—at least that's the way he looks this Century.

MARIA TERESA: *That* was Lucifer?

VLAD: The Son of Morning!

LIZZIE: In the flesh!

DON JUAN: I feel so…violated.

(VLAD *grabs* SIMON.)

VLAD: Ah, what the hell—whose afraid of the Devil? We have the best lawyer in Hell!

MARIA TERESA: We have the *only* lawyer in Hell.

SIMON: Maybe I'll start a trend!

ALL: Don't count on it.

VLAD: To Simon!

ALL: To Simon!

SIMON: So you're not surprised I got a handshake from Lucifer?

VLAD: I didn't say that. I am surprised…I'm surprised he didn't give you an open mouth kiss! To "No further questions!"

ALL: No…further…questions!

(Spotlight on SIMON, *who suddenly breaks into the opening refrain of* All Of Me:*)*

SIMON: "All of me, *why not* take all of me?"

*(*SIMON *dances amongst the Hellions in an easy swing as he continues to sing…)*

SIMON: "Can't you see, I'm not good without you. Take my lips—I want to lose them; take these arms—I'll never use them…"

*(*GOD *enters, with the* INTERVIEWER:*)*

GOD: "Your goodbye left me with eyes that cry. How can I get along without you?"

(The tavern folk sing in harmony as GOD *crosses to them, seeking consolation.)*

ALL: "You took the part that once was my heart—so why not, why not take all of me?"

(The INTERVIEWER *sings directly to the audience, as the tavern dances behind, keeping the beat.)*

INTERVIEWER: "All of me! Come on, get all of me! Can't you see, I'm just a mess, without you. You got lips—speak out and use them; look at those strong arms—use them or lose them!" *(Singling out the audience)* "Your goodbye, yes yours,"

TAVERN: "Yours!"

INTERVIEWER: "Left me with eyes that cry. How can I-"

TAVERN: "How can *we*?"

INTERVIEWER: "—ever make it—

ALL: "—without you?"

(He returns to the tavern crowd.)

INTERVIEWER: "Your favorite part—used to be my heart! So why not? *(Calls out)* Everybody!

ALL: "Why not take all of me!"

(They arrange themselves into a final tableau, as a huge banner drops from above, proclaiming:)

("GO TO HELL!")

(Confetti falls.)

(Blackout)

END OF PLAY

...But not The Struggle...